SECOND EDITION

Super Practice Book

2

T0303271

SUPER PRACTICE

Emma Szlachta · Garan Holcombe

CAMBRIDGE
UNIVERSITY PRESS

Map of the book

There's / There are

The classroom is in a mess. Let's tidy.

Good idea.

There are some pencils and some pens ...

... and **there are** some books. Let's put them on the bookcase.

There's a ball. Let's put it in the cupboard.

Thank you. That's fantastic!

Language focus

Use **there is** / **there's** and **there are** to say what singular and plural nouns you can see.

***There's** a car.* ***There are** some balls.*

1 Look and match.

a   some

2 Write *is* or *are*.

1 There ___is___ a red book.

2 There _____ some pencils.

3 There _____ an apple.

4 There _____ a clock.

5 There _____ some sweets.

6 There _____ a green pen.

3 Write *There are some* or *There is a*.

1 ___There are some___ kites.

2 _____ doll.

3 _____ monster.

4 _____ planes.

5 _____ car.

6 _____ balls.

Imperatives

It's good to see you all again. **Stand** up, please.

Don't open your books.

Put your pens in your pencil case. Let's play a game.

Language focus

Use **imperatives** to give instructions.

Stand up.	*Don't* stand up.
Sit down.	*Don't* sit down.
Put your book in your bag.	*Don't* close your books.

1   **Read and complete the sentences.**

1 Open ___your books__ .

2 Sit _____.

3 Stand _____.

4 C_____ your bag.

5 Pass me y_____r ru_____r.

6 Don't o_____ y_____r bags.

2 Complete the dialogue with the words from the box.

Pass   open   down   Don't   up   ~~sit~~

Mrs Brown Hello, class. Welcome back! It's good to see you all again. OK,
(1) _____sit_____ down please and (2) _____ your books.

Matt Oh no! I haven't got a pencil! (3) _____ me a pencil,
please, Sally.

Sally Shhh, Matt. Here you are.

Matt Mrs Brown, I can't see the board.

Mrs Brown Stand (4) _____,
Matt. (5) _____
sit down there. Sit
(6) _____ here.

Matt Thank you.

3 Write the instructions.

1 Don't sit down.
2 _____
3 _____
4 _____
5 _____
6 _____

Reading: a poem

1 Read the poem and write *t* (true) or *f* (false).

A poem about my desk

The classroom is a mess.

Look at my desk!

There are some pens and a book.

An apple and a clock.

There are some pencils and a sausage!

A sausage? A sausage!

Don't sit down, Sue and Dan.

Put the pencils in your pencil case
and the sausage in your bag.

Don't sit down, Anna and Alex.

Put the clock on the wall
and the apple in your desk.

Don't sit down – let's tidy this mess.

1 The classroom isn't tidy. [t]

2 There are two books. ☐

3 There's a banana. ☐

4 There's a clock. ☐

5 There are some pencils. ☐

6 There isn't a sausage. ☐

Writing

1 **What is on your desk? Write a list.**

There's a _____

There are some _____

2 **Write a poem about your desk, then draw it.**

A poem about my desk

The classroom is a mess.

Look at my desk!

There are _____

_____

_____

_____

_____

Look at my desk!

Don't sit down – let's tidy this mess.

Listening: in the classroom

1 🎧 01 Listen and number the pictures.

a ☐

b ☐

c ☐

d Good morning, class! ☐

e ☐

f ☐

2 🎧 02 Listen and tick ✓ the correct sentences.

☐ Sit down, please.
☐ Stand up, please.
☐ Get your books, please.
☐ Get your crayons, please.
☐ Write your name, please.

✓ Don't sit down, please.
☐ Don't stand up.
☐ Don't get your books.
☐ Don't get your crayons.
☐ Don't write your name.

1 **What's in your bag? Draw five things and say.**

There's a pencil case. There are three books. There's a notebook.

2 **Work with a friend. Talk about your bags.**
Play the memory game.

There's a pencil case in your bag.

Yes! What colour is it?

It's blue.

Yes, that's right!

3 **Talk about your friend's bag.**

In Pablo's bag, there's a blue pencil case. There are three books – one is yellow …

1 Telling the time

Use **What's the time?** to ask the time and **It's ... o'clock** to answer.

Use **When do you ... ?** to ask about the time of an activity, and **At ... o'clock** to answer.

What's the time?	*It's nine o'clock.*
When do you have breakfast?	*At seven o'clock.*

1 Read and match.

1 What's the time? It's two o'clock. **b**

2 When do you have lunch? At twelve o'clock. ☐

3 What's the time? It's ten o'clock. ☐

4 When do you go to bed? At eight o'clock. ☐

5 What's the time? It's four o'clock. ☐

6 When do you get up? At six o'clock. ☐

2 Complete the dialogue with the words from the box.

~~time~~   ten   do   When   at   o'clock

Mary   Tell me about your day. What (1) _____**time**_____ do you get up?

Alan   OK. Well, I get up (2) _____ seven o'clock.

Mary   (3) _____ do you go to school?

Alan   At nine (4) _____ .

Mary   And when (5) _____ you play in the park?

Alan   On Saturday at (6) _____ o'clock.

3 Write sentences.

1 I ____**get up at**____
____**six o'clock**____ .

2 I _____
_____ .

3 I _____
_____ .

4 I _____
_____ .

5 I _____
_____ .

6 I _____
_____ .

Present simple, 3rd person

Eva **gets up** at seven o'clock.

She **goes** to school at eight o'clock.

She **has** lunch at twelve o'clock.

She **brushes** her teeth and then she **goes** to bed at eight o'clock.

Language focus

Use the **present simple, 3rd person (gets, goes)** to talk about what other people do.

*Eva **gets up** at seven o'clock.*   *She **goes** to school at eight o'clock.*

1 **Match the sentences with the pictures.**

1 He has dinner at six o'clock with his family. `d`

2 He goes to work at eight o'clock at night. ☐

3 He comes home at six o'clock in the morning. ☐

4 He has breakfast at seven o'clock. ☐

5 He plays in the park at eight o'clock. ☐

6 He goes to bed at nine o'clock in the evening. ☐

a

b

c

d

e

f

2 Match to complete the sentences.

1 Emma gets   a   breakfast and
                 brushes her teeth.

2 Kate has   b   to bed at eight o'clock.

3 Dan gets   c   her teeth in the morning and in the evening.

4 Hugo goes   d   up at nine o'clock on Saturdays and she plays football.

5 Lucy brushes   e   in the park after school.

6 Fred plays   f   dressed in jeans and a T-shirt.

3 Complete the text with the words from the box.

| has   leaves   arrives   gets   starts   ~~works~~ |

Alison is a teacher. She
(1) ___**works**___ in a big school in
New York. In the morning, she
(2) _____ the house at seven
o'clock and (3) _____ at
school at eight o'clock. She
(4) _____ two classes in the
morning and then she has lunch.
She (5) _____ her afternoon
class at one o'clock and the children
go home at four o'clock. She leaves
school at six o'clock and
(6) _____ home and has
dinner. What a long day!

Reading: a blog entry

1 Read the text. Circle the correct words.

My Blog
by Suzy James

My Mum

My mum is fantastic! She gets up at six o'clock and walks me and my brother to school at eight o'clock. Then she goes to work on the bus. She has a busy day at work and she has lunch at her desk. Then at four o'clock she gets me and my brother from school and she helps me with my school work. She cooks and we all have dinner at five o'clock. On Fridays we have pizza – it's my favourite dinner. I go to bed at eight o'clock and Mum goes to bed at ten o'clock – she has a long day.

1 Mum gets up at *six* / *eight* o'clock.

2 She *walks* / *goes by bus* to work.

3 She has lunch at *her desk* / *one o'clock*.

4 She *works some more* / *helps Suzy with her work* at home.

5 *Mum has* / *They all have* dinner at five o'clock.

6 *Suzy* / *Mum* goes to bed at ten o'clock.

1 Write notes about your mum or dad. Use the words from the box.

> ~~get up~~   have breakfast   go to work   have lunch
> start work   leave work   get home   watch TV   go to bed

Dad gets up at seven o'clock.

2 Write about your mum or dad. What does she / he do?

My Blog

Listening: daily routines

1 🎧 03 **Listen and tick ☑ the correct clock.**

1 Eva gets up at … ☑ ☐

2 Eva has breakfast at … ☐ ☐

3 Eva goes to school at … ☐ ☐

4 Eva has lunch at … ☐ ☐

5 Eva has dinner at … ☐ ☐

6 Eva goes to bed at … ☐ ☐

2 🎧 04 **Listen and circle *yes* or *no*.**

1 Dan gets home at four o'clock.   (yes)/ no

2 Dan walks home with his mum
  and his sister.   *yes / no*

3 At five o'clock, Dan plays with his sister.   *yes / no*

4 Dan has dinner at seven o'clock.   *yes / no*

5 After dinner, Dan, his sister and
  his dad read a story.   *yes / no*

6 After the story, Dan brushes his teeth
  and goes to bed.   *yes / no*

1 Look at Mindy's day. Choose a picture and say. Play the guessing game.

> Mindy has dinner at seven o'clock.

> Number 5!

get up

have breakfast

have lunch

play in the park

have dinner

go to bed

2 Draw a picture of your favourite activity at the weekend. Complete and practise.

At the weekend, I _____ at _____ o'clock. It's my favourite activity!

3 Show your picture to a friend. Talk about your favourite activity at the weekend.

> Look, this is me at the weekend. I play computer games at five o'clock. What about you?

> I ride my bike in the park. I go there at eleven o'clock.

2 Likes / Doesn't like

Eva **likes** a sandwich at lunchtime. She **doesn't like** cheese in her sandwich. She **likes** sausages.

Eva **likes** a banana and orange juice for breakfast.

Eva has dinner at five o'clock. She **likes** chicken and carrots. She **doesn't like** peas.

Eva has supper at seven o'clock. She **likes** a glass of milk and cookies.

Language focus

Use **likes** and **doesn't like** to talk about preferences.

*Freddy **likes** spiders.*   *Freddy **doesn't like** apples.*

1 Circle the correct words to complete the sentences.

1 Tony *likes* / *doesn't like* carrots.

2 Ben *likes* / *doesn't like* apples.

3 Mary *likes* / *doesn't like* cheese.

4 Monica *likes* / *doesn't like* bananas.

5 Bill *likes* / *doesn't like* peas.

6 Tim *likes* / *doesn't like* chicken.

a
b
c
d
e
f

2 Complete the text with the words from the box.

likes   ~~likes~~   doesn't   likes   likes   like

The zoo is busy. There are lots of animals. It's six o'clock and the animals are having breakfast. The zebra **(1)** _____**likes**_____ apples but he **(2)** _____ like bananas. The monkey **(3)** _____ lovely yellow bananas for breakfast and the tiger **(4)** _____ steak. The snake doesn't **(5)** _____ peas – he **(6)** _____ a big rat for breakfast. Yum!

3 Complete the sentences.

1 Emma **doesn't like carrots** .

2 Mark _____ .

3 Suzy _____ .

4 Dan _____ .

5 Pam _____ .

6 Toby _____ .

Does ... like ... ?

Language focus

Use **Does ... like ... ?** to ask questions about what people like.

Use **Yes, he / she does** and **No, he / she doesn't** to give short answers.

Does Mark **like** bananas?   **Yes, he does. / No, he doesn't.**

1   **Write *Yes, he / she does* or *No, he / she doesn't*.**

1 Does Anna like sausages? ___**Yes, she does**___. They're her favourite.

2 Does Bill walk to school? _____. He rides his bike.

3 Does May like cats? _____. She likes dogs.

4 Does your mum get up at six o'clock? _____ but not at the weekend.

5 Does your parrot like carrots? _____. He likes apples.

6 Does your dad go to work every day? _____. He arrives at nine o'clock.

2 Complete the dialogue with the words from the box.

he   ~~Does~~   walk   she   does   doesn't

Toby (1) ___Does___ your mum get up early?

Katy Yes, (2) _____ does.
She goes to work every day.

Toby Does she (3) _____ to work?

Katy No, she (4) _____. She rides a bike.

Toby Does she have lunch at work?

Katy Yes, she (5) _____. She has a sandwich and some fruit.

Toby Does your dad ride a bike to work, too?

Katy No, (6) _____ doesn't. He goes by car.

3 Write questions and answers.

1 sausages / Mark / Does / like / ?
___Does Mark like sausages?___ ✓ ___Yes, he does.___

2 ride / Ben / school / a bike / Does / to / ?
_____ ✓ _____

3 chicken / the zebra / eat / Does / ?
_____ ✗ _____

4 Does / swimming / like / the hippo / ?
_____ ✗ _____

5 a lot / cat / your / Does / sleep / ?
_____ ✓ _____

6 eight o'clock / Tina / go to / Does / bed / at / ?
_____ ✗ _____

Reading: a web page

1 **Read the text and answer the questions.**

Home | **Our animals** | **Contact us** | **Opening times**

BLUEWATER ZOO

The Hippos

This is Hugo the hippo. He's 15 years old and lives at the zoo. He's from Africa. He's got a big house and water to swim in. He gets up early in the morning but he likes a sleep after lunch. He likes fruit and his favourite food is apples but he doesn't like carrots! Does he like the water? Yes, he does – and he can swim.

Hannah lives with Hugo. Hugo and Hannah are good friends. Hannah likes the water too but she doesn't like apples – she likes bananas. Come and visit Hugo and Hannah! We are open from nine o'clock to five o'clock every day.

1 Where is Hugo from?   He's from Africa.

2 Does Hugo get up early?   _____

3 Does he sleep in the morning? _____

4 What's his favourite food? _____

5 Can Hugo swim? _____

6 Does Hannah like the water? _____

1 **Write notes about Terry the tiger. Use the words from the box.**

eight   a long tail   ~~India~~   steak   carrots   run fast

Terry comes from (1) _____India_____.
He's (2) _____ years old.
He likes (3) _____.
He doesn't like (4) _____.
He can (5) _____.
He's got (6) _____.

2 **Write about Terry the tiger. Use your notes from Activity 1.**

_____

_____

_____

_____

_____

_____

_____

_____

_____

Listening: my favourite animal

1 🎧 **05** Listen and match the children with the animals they like.

1 Alex
2 Grace
3 Tom
4 Kim
5 Jill
6 Nick

a
b
c
d
e
f

2 🎧 **06** Listen and circle the correct answers.

1 Does Holly's mum like crocodiles?   **ⓐ** Yes, she does.   **b** No, she doesn't.

2 Does her dad like zebras?   **a** Yes, he does.   **b** No, he doesn't.

3 Does her brother like snakes?   **a** Yes, he does.   **b** No, he doesn't.

4 Does her sister like snakes?   **a** Yes, she does.   **b** No, she doesn't.

5 Does Holly like parrots?   **a** Yes, she does.   **b** No, she doesn't.

6 Does Holly like monkeys?   **a** Yes, she does.   **b** No, she doesn't.

1 **Work with a friend. Look at the photos. Play the guessing game.**

monkey

Does it live in trees?

Yes, it does.

Can it fly?

No, it can't.

elephant

Is it the monkey?

Yes, it is!

parrot

bear

spider

fish

2 **With your friend, talk about the animals in Activity 1.**

Do you like monkeys?

Yes, I do! Do you like elephants?

3 **Which animals does your friend like or not like? Say.**

Emma likes monkeys, but she doesn't like parrots. She really likes bears and …

3 Has ... got ... ?

> **Has** your town **got** a hospital?

> **Has** your town **got** a cinema?

> No, it hasn't.

> Yes, it has.

Language focus

Use **Has ... got ... ?** to ask about possessions and places.

Use **Yes, it has** and **No, it hasn't** to give short answers.

Has your town *got* a swimming pool?   *Yes, it has.*

Has your town *got* a train station?   *No, it hasn't.*

---

1   **Write *Yes, he has* or *No, he hasn't*.**

1 Has Ben got a book?   <u>**Yes, he has.**</u>

2 Has he got a bike? _____

3 Has he got a cat? _____

4 Has he got a notebook? _____

5 Has he got a kite? _____

6 Has he got a jacket? _____

Ben

2 **Look and write questions and answers.**

1 __Has Top Town got__ a train station?   Yes, it has.

2 Has Top Town got a school?   _____.

3 _____ a hospital?   No, it hasn't.

4 Has Top Town got a café?   _____.

5 Has Top Town got a park?   _____.

6 _____ a swimming pool?   No, it hasn't.

3 **Write questions and answers.**

1 town / your / Has / a cinema / got / ?

__Has your town got a cinema?__ ✓ __Yes, it has.__

2 your / a shop / Has / town / got / ?

_____ ✓ _____

3 a dog / Anna / got / Has / ?

_____ ✗ _____

4 Tim / a go-kart / got / Has / ?

_____ ✗ _____

5 a playground / Has / got / your town / ?

_____ ✓ _____

6 your town / a hospital / got / Has / ?

_____ ✗ _____

Prepositions

Where is the cinema?

It's **between** the café and the fruit shop.

Use **prepositions** to describe where things and places are.

*The cinema is **between** the toy shop and Green Street.*

*The hospital is **behind** the playground.*

*The school is **in front of** the park.*

*The café is **next to** the train station.*

1 **Circle the correct words to complete the sentences.**

1 The books are *next to* / *behind* the apple.

2 The apple is *in front of* / *between* the books and the pencils.

3 The ruler is *in front of* / *behind* the clock.

4 The fish is *on* / *in* the water.

5 The red book is *between* / *next to* the fish and the clock.

6 The blue book is *on* / *under* the yellow book.

2 **Match the sentences with the pictures.**

1 The cat is next to the dog.   `e`

2 The cat is in front of the dog.   ☐

3 The cat is between the dog
and the ball.   ☐

4 The cat is on the ball.   ☐

5 The cat is behind the ball.   ☐

6 The cat is under the ball.   ☐

3 **Look and write the words.**

1 The school is _____**next to**_____ the café.

2 The car is _____ the café.

3 The café is _____ the cinema.

4 The train is _____ the train station.

5 The tree is _____ the cinema.

6 The café is _____ the school and the cinema.

Reading: a letter

1 **Read the text. Circle the correct words.**

Hi James

My favourite days of the week are Saturday and
Sunday. On Saturday my mum takes me and my
brother to the swimming pool in the morning. We go
every week and we have lots of fun. After that we go to
the café next to the swimming pool for our lunch. I have
a sandwich and my brother has a pizza. On Sundays we
go to the park behind our house and we play football
and sometimes we go to the cinema in town. It isn't
a big cinema, but it shows films for children on Sunday
mornings. My favourite films are about animals.

Has your town got a swimming pool? What's your
favourite day of the week?

Freddie

1 Freddie (likes) / *doesn't like* the weekend.

2 Freddie goes to the *cinema* / *swimming pool* on Saturday mornings.

3 He eats *a pizza* / *a sandwich* for lunch.

4 The park is behind *the cinema* / *his house.*

5 The cinema *is* / *isn't* small.

6 Freddie *likes* / *doesn't like* films about animals.

1 Write a list of places in your town. What can you do there?

_____

_____

_____

_____

_____

_____

_____

2 Write a letter to Freddie. Tell him about your favourite days and where you go in your town.

_____

_____

_____

_____

_____

_____

_____

Listening: places

1 🎧 07 Listen and tick ✓ or cross ✗.

Places	Sam's town	Hugo's town
1	✓	
2		
3		
4		
5		

2 🎧 08 Listen and draw lines.

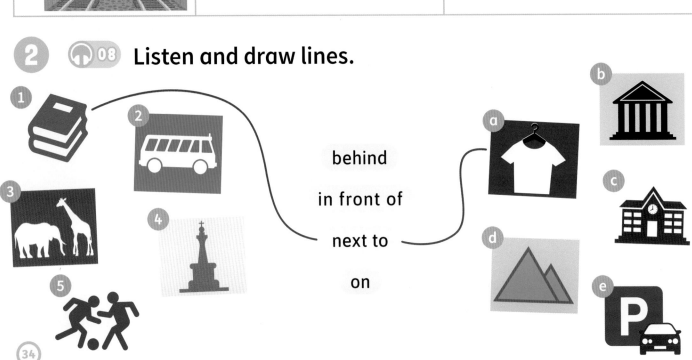

behind

in front of

next to

on

34

1 **Choose five places to complete the map of the town. Give your town a name.**

sports centre
museum
train station
swimming pool
market
cinema
hospital
playground

Name of town: _____

2 **Work with a friend. Which places has your friend's town got? Ask and tick ✓ your friend's town's places in Activity 1.**

What's the name of your town?

It's Super Town.

Has your town got a sports centre?

No, it hasn't. Has your town got a hospital?

Yes, it has.

3 **Work with a friend. Where are the places on your maps? Ask and answer.**

Where's the sports centre in your town?

It's next to the train station.

4 Would you like ... ?

Would you like a sandwich?

Yes, please.

Would you like some tomatoes?

No, thank you.

Would you like a mango?

No, thank you.

Would you like some grapes?

Yes, please.

Language focus

Use **Would you like ... ?** to ask polite questions. Use **Yes, please** and **No, thank you** to give polite short answers.

Would you like a tomato?   **Yes, please.**

Would you like some bread?   **No, thank you.**

1 Look and write *some* or *an*.

1 __some__ watermelon   5 _____ apple

2 _____ egg   6 _____ mango

3 _____ cake   7 _____ bread

4 _____ grapes

2 Complete the dialogue with the words from the box.

a   some   please   ~~like~~   Would   No

Dad Would you (1) **like** a sandwich, Sally?

Sally Yes, (2) _____.

Dad (3) _____ you like a sausage in your sandwich?

Sally (4) _____, thank you. I'd like (5) _____ cheese.

Dad Would you like an apple or (6) _____ banana, too?

Sally Yes, please – a banana.

3 Look and write questions and answers.

1 **Would you like a mango?** ✓ Yes, please.

2 _____ some grapes? ✗

No, _____.

3 _____ apple? ✗

_____ thank you.

4 _____ ? ✓

Yes, _____.

5 _____ ? ✓

_____.

6 _____ ? ✗

_____.

ⓐ   ⓑ

ⓒ   ⓓ

ⓔ   ⓕ

Are there / Is there any ... ?

Is there any milk in the fridge?

No, there isn't.

Are there any lemons?

No, there aren't any.

Is there any chicken in the fridge?

Yes, there is.

Language focus

Use **Is there any ... ?** and **Are there any ... ?** to ask about singular and plural nouns. Use **Yes, there is / are** and **No, there isn't / aren't any** to give short answers.

Are there any pears in the fridge?   ***Yes, there are.***

No, there aren't any.

Is there any bread in the basket?   ***Yes, there is.***

No, there isn't any.

1   **Look and write.**

1 Are there any bananas? <u>No, there aren't any.</u>

2 Is there any bread? _____

3 Are there any tomatoes? _____

4 Is there any fish? _____

5 Are there any grapes? _____

6 Are there any pears? _____

2 Write numbers to put the dialogue in order.

Mia — Are there any sausages? ☐

John — Yes, there are. There are two sausages. ☐

John — Yes, there is. There's white bread. Let's look in the fridge. ☐

Mia — OK. Is there any chicken? ☐

Mia — My favourite – a sausage sandwich. Is there any cake? ☐

John — Yes, there is. There's chocolate cake. Yummy! ☐

Mia — Let's make sandwiches for lunch. Is there any bread? 1

John — No, there isn't any. ☐

3 Write questions.

1 Are / any / there / potatoes / the basket / in / ?

Are there any potatoes in the basket?

2 there / Is / cake / any / ?

_____

3 there / lemons / Are / any / ?

_____

4 there / cheese / in / Is / the fridge / any / ?

_____

5 the basket / Is / any / bread / there / in / ?

_____

6 there / Are / apples / in / the fridge / any / ?

_____

Reading: a recipe

1 **Look, then answer the questions about the recipe.**

milk   butter   lemon   chocolate

egg   flour   frying pan

PANCAKES

1. Put a cup of flour in a bowl.
2. Put an egg and a cup of milk in the bowl. Start mixing.
3. Put one spoon of butter in a frying pan.
4. Put some of the mixture in the frying pan.
5. Fry the pancake for two minutes each side. (Can you throw the pancake?!)
6. Put chocolate, fruit or lemon juice on your pancake.

Enjoy the pancakes with your friends.

1 How many cups of flour are there? **There is one cup of flour.** _____

2 How many eggs are there? _____

3 Is there any water? _____

4 Is there any butter? _____

5 Is there any fruit? _____

6 What else can you put on the pancake? _____

1 What food would you like to make? Write a list of things you would need to make it.

_____

_____

_____

_____

_____

_____

_____

_____

_____

2 Write a recipe for your food.

_____

_____

_____

_____

_____

_____

Listening: fruit, vegetables and eggs!

1 🎧 09 **Listen and number the pictures.**

a

☐

b

☐

c

☐

d

☐

e

1

f

☐

2 🎧 10 **What would they like? Listen and match.**

1 Lucy

2 Connor

3 Anna

4 Jack

5 May

a

b

c

d

e

1 **What have you got for your picnic? Draw five things and say.**

For my picnic, there are some sandwiches, some grapes, some crisps and some tomatoes. To drink, there's some juice.

2 **Work with a friend. Talk about your picnic food and drink.**

There are some sandwiches for my picnic.

How many sandwiches are there?

There are three sandwiches.

3 **What would your friend like at your picnic?**
Ask and answer.

Would you like a sandwich?

Yes, please! Would you like an apple?

No, thank you. I don't like apples.

5 This, that, these, those

Language focus

Use **this** and **these** to talk about singular (this) and plural (these) things that are near to you. Use **that** and **those** to talk about singular (that) and plural (those) things that are far from you.

*I like **this** book.*   *I like **that** book.*

*I like **these** books.*   *I like **those** books.*

1 Circle the correct words to complete the sentences.

1 I like (this) / these lamp.

2 I don't like these / this yellow chairs.

3 Do you like these / those blue chairs?

4 I like that / those lamp.

5 I like these / this blue jeans.

6 Do you like that / this red cap?

2 Match the sentences with the pictures.

1 I like this hat. `e`

2 I don't like these shoes. ☐

3 I like those shoes. ☐

4 I don't like that jacket. ☐

5 I don't like that hat. ☐

6 I like this jacket. ☐

a

b

c

d

e

f

3 Look and write *this*, *that*, *these* or *those*.

Do you like **(1)** ___**these**___ yellow shoes?

No, I don't. I like **(2)** _____ green shoes.

Look at **(3)** _____ hats over there.

Do you like **(4)** _____ red hat?

Yes, I do.

I like **(5)** _____ red T-shirt. Do you?

Yes, I do. I like this blue shirt, too.

Do you like **(6)** _____ shoes over there?

No, I don't. They're awful!

Whose ... is this? / Whose ... are these?

Use **Whose ... are these?** to ask about possession of plural items.

Use **Whose ... is this?** to ask about possession of singular items.

Whose socks are these?	*They're Fred's.*
Whose hat is this?	*It's May's.*

1 Circle the correct words to complete the sentences.

1 A Whose cap is this?

   B It's *Claire* / (Claire's).

2 A Whose socks are *these* / *this*?

   B They're Bob's.

3 A Whose pencil is this?

   B It's *my* / *mine*.

4 Whose jeans are these? Are they *yours* / *your*?

5 *Whose* / *Who's* doll is this? Is it Jane's?

6 Whose football boots are these? Are they *Tom's* / *Toms*?

2 **Look and write the names.**

1 Whose purple socks are those?   They're May's.

2 Whose football is that?   _____

3 Whose plane is that?   _____

4 Whose hat is that?   _____

5 Whose black socks are those?   _____

6 Whose white shoes are those?   _____

3 **Complete the dialogue with the words from the box.**

they're   ~~Whose~~   yours   mine   's   these

Mrs Bush   What a mess! Let's tidy the classroom. **(1)** ____Whose____ pen is this?

Tim   It's **(2)** _____, Mrs Bush.

Mrs Bush   And whose pencil case is this? Is it **(3)** _____, Alice?

Alice   No, it's not mine. It's Tim **(4)** _____.

Mrs Bush   OK. Whose socks are **(5)** _____ under the desk? Are they yours, Tim?

Tim   Sorry, Mrs Bush. Yes, **(6)** _____ mine.

Mrs Bush   Tim! Please tidy up your pen, your pencil case and your socks!

Reading: a web page

1 Read the texts and answer the questions.

HOME IDEAS

Home | Bedrooms | Living rooms | Garden | Contact us

When I want to think, I go to my bedroom. It's my favourite room in the house. My room is blue and green and I've got lots of books. I like books. I haven't got a TV or a computer in my bedroom but that's OK. I can watch TV in the living room. I listen to music in my bedroom and it's a great place to have fun! Look at those blue, green and red things on the wall – I can climb in my bedroom!

Alice from England

Ben from Canada

My bedroom is blue. I've got some toys and that's my sister's doll on my bed! I haven't got a clock or a bookcase. Can you see that big brown tree on the wall? I look at my tree when I want to think about my holidays. I like climbing trees. I've got a cat, Bobby, and he doesn't like the tree! There isn't water in my bedroom, but my bed is a boat!

1 There's a boat. Whose bedroom is it? **It's Ben's bedroom.**

2 Whose bedroom has got a tree in it? _____

3 Whose bedroom is green and blue? _____

4 It hasn't got a TV. Whose bedroom is it? _____

5 Whose bedroom can you climb in? _____

6 There are toys. Whose bedroom is it? _____

1 What is there in your bedroom? Write a list.

_____   _____

_____   _____

_____   _____

_____   _____

_____   _____

2 Draw and write about your bedroom. What do you like doing there?

Listening: the perfect room

1 🎧 **11** Listen and tick ☑ the correct picture.

2 🎧 **12** Listen and circle *Adam's* or *Lucy's*.

1 Whose ball is this? *Adam's / (Lucy's)*

2 Whose crayons are these? *Adam's / Lucy's*

3 Whose jeans are these? *Adam's / Lucy's*

4 Whose jacket is this? *Adam's / Lucy's*

5 Whose books are these? *Adam's / Lucy's*

6 Whose kite is this? *Adam's / Lucy's*

1 Draw five things that belong to people in your family. You can draw clothes, toys, furniture or other things.

2 Work with a friend. Look at your pictures in Activity 1. Ask and answer.

Whose mirror is this?

It's my sister's mirror. Whose shoes are these?

They're my dad's shoes.

3 Talk about your friend's pictures.

My friend is Sue and this is her sister's mirror. It's beautiful. These are her dad's shoes. They're brown. This …

6 Am / Is / Are + adjective

Language focus

Use **Are you** + **adjective?** to ask about how people are feeling.

Use **I'm** + **adjective** to describe how you are feeling.

Are you angry?   *No, I'm not angry.* ***I'm tired.***

Are you happy?   *Yes, I'm happy and* ***I'm excited.***

1 Look, read and write the words.

1 He is __sad__.

2 She is _____.

3 She is _____.

4 He is _____.

5 She is _____.

6 He is _____.

2 Match the phrases with the pictures.

1 I'm excited.
2 I'm sad.
3 I'm tired.
4 I'm happy.
5 I'm angry.
6 I'm scared.

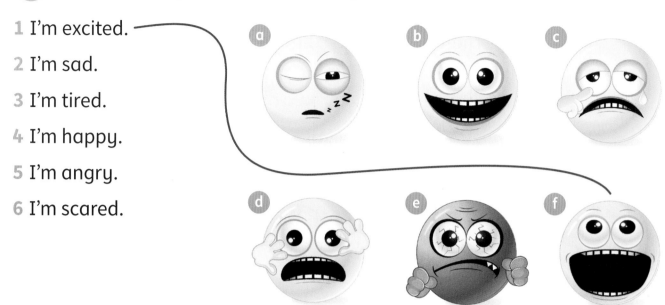

3 Circle the correct words to complete the sentences.

1 Are you angry?
   No, I'm not. It's a busy week.
   I'm (tired) / sad.

2 Are you excited / scared?
   Yes, there's a big dog. Help!

3 Are you angry / happy?
   Yes, I am. It's the weekend!

4 Are you sad?
   No, I'm not. I'm angry / excited. There isn't any cake.

5 Are you excited / tired?
   Yes, I am. It's my birthday party today!

6 Are you tired?
   No, I'm not. I'm happy / sad. I can't play football today.

The months, our, their

Thank you! **Our** birthdays are both in May.

I've got an invitation for Sally and Tim, too.

When are **their** birthdays?

Come to Lucy's **Party**
Saturday 26th May
12 Green Road
3 O'clock

Yes! My party is at my house!

Sally's birthday is in July and Tim's birthday is in October.

Language focus

Use **our** and **their** before nouns to talk about plural possession.

Our birthdays are both in May.

Their birthdays are in November.

1 Look and write the months.

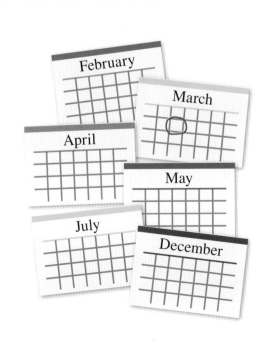

1 My birthday is in <u>M</u> <u>a</u> r <u>c</u> h.

2 Our birthdays are in __ e __ __ __ m b __ r.

3 My cat is four. Its birthday is in A __ __ __ i __.

4 My dog is ten. Its birthday is in __ __ l __.

5 Their birthdays are in F __ __ __ r __ __ r __.

6 His birthday is in __ a __.

2 Circle the correct words to complete the sentences.

1 It's Lucy's birthday today. (Her) / Their birthday is in May.

2 It's Ben's party today. He's nine. *His / He* birthday is in August.

3 My sister is fifteen today. *She / Her* birthday is in May.

4 I've got a present for my dad. *Her / His* birthday is in October.

5 We are eight today! *Our / Their* birthday is in December.

6 I'm ten today. *My / Mine* birthday is in January.

3 Complete the sentences with the words from the box.

| Her His Its My ~~Our~~ Their |

1 We are seven. _____**Our**_____ birthdays are in March.

2 I'm four. _____ birthday's today.

3 She's ten. _____ birthday party is today.

4 He's twelve. _____ party is at four o'clock.

5 They are six today. _____ birthday is in July.

6 My dog is five today. _____ birthday is in April.

Reading: an invitation

1 Read the party invitations. Answer the questions.

Dear Jenny

Please come to my party on Sunday 14th July at one o'clock. My party is in the park. Please bring your swimming things – we can swim in the swimming pool. I've got a football so we can play football, too. My mum has got lots of nice food – sandwiches, sweets and cupcakes!

See you on Sunday.

Katy

Dear Ben

We are seven! Come to our party on Saturday. It starts at four o'clock. It's at Dan's house – 45 West Road (near the swimming pool). We can play games and eat birthday cake.

Don't be late.

See you there!

Dan and Ruby

1 What time is Katy's party? **It's at one o'clock.**

2 What month is Katy's party? _____

3 What can you do at Katy's party? _____

4 How old are Dan and Ruby? _____

5 Whose house is Dan and Ruby's party at? _____

6 Where is Dan's house? _____

1 Make notes about your party.

When?	What time?	Where?	Activities?	Food?
		park	painting football	sandwiches

2 Write an invitation. Use your notes from Activity 1.

Listening: parties

1 🎧 13 **Listen and number the pictures.**

a ☐

b ☐

c ☐

d ☐

e **1**

f ☐

2 🎧 14 **Listen and draw lines.**

1 Alex and Dan

2 Kim

3 Pat and Mark

4 Bobby

5 Olivia and Alice

a

b

c

d

e

1 **Work with a friend. Plan a class party. Complete the table.**

> Let's bring some balloons to our party.

> OK. And I'd like to bring some grapes, too.

> Good idea!

Things	Food and drink	Games
balloons	grapes	bingo

2 **With your friend, write your answers. Then practise.**

1 Where is your class party?

It's _____.

2 What month is your party?

It's in _____.

3 What day is your party?

It's on _____.

4 What do you want to do?

We want to play _____
and _____.

3 **Talk about your class party.**

> Our party is in the classroom. It's in April and it's on Friday. We want to play with balloons, eat cake and sing.

7 I'd like to ...

I'd like to go sailing on a big boat.

I'd like to fly to Canada and see a bear.

I'd like to drive a big lorry.

Language focus

Use **I'd like to** + **verb ...** to talk about wishes.

I'd like to go to Africa by plane.

I'd like to drive a train.

1 Complete the sentences with the words from the box.

like ~~to~~ to see I'd fly around eat

1. I'd like to go ___**to**___ Canada.

2. I'd _____ to see a snake.

3. _____ like to go to Italy.

4. I'd like to _____ ice cream.

5. I'd like to _____ the world.

6. I'd like _____ a bear.

2 Circle the correct words to complete the sentences.

1 I'd like to (go) / sail to the jungle by bus.

2 I'd like / likes to eat a pizza.

3 I like / 'd like to see an elephant.

4 I'd like to fly to / fly Africa.

5 I'd like sail / to sail around the world.

6 I'd like to drive / fly a bus.

3 Write sentences using *I'd like to* and the words from the box.

> ride a scooter   fly a helicopter   sail a boat
> ~~drive a train~~   ride a motorbike   drive a lorry

1 **I'd like to drive a train.**

2 _____

3 _____

4 _____

5 _____

6 _____

verb + ing

What **are** you **doing? Are** you **driving** a car?

No, I'm not.

What **are** you **doing? Are** you **flying** a plane?

No, I'm not.

Are you **driving** a big lorry?

Yes, I am!

Yes, I am!

Are you **skateboarding?**

Language focus

Use **is** / **are** + **verb** + **ing** to ask and answer about actions at the moment of speaking. Use **Yes, I am** and **No, I'm not** to give short answers.

*What **are** you **doing?***	*I**'m flying** a plane.*
*What **is** he **doing?***	*He**'s riding** his bike.*
***Are** you **flying** a plane?*	***Yes, I am.** / **No, I'm not.***

1 **Write *ing* words.**

1 She <u>'s</u> <u>listening</u> to music. (listen)

2 He _____ _____ breakfast. (eat)

3 I _____ _____ dressed. (get)

4 She _____ _____ an ice cream. (eat)

5 He _____ _____ his teeth. (brush)

6 I _____ _____ a photo. (take)

7

2 Write questions.

1 are / What / doing / you / ?

  What are you doing?

2 football / you / Are / playing / ?

  _____

3 she / Is / a scooter / riding / ?

  _____

4 is / What / doing / she / ?

  _____

5 an ice cream / Are / eating / you / ?

  _____

6 playing / he / Is / computer games / ?

  _____

3 Look and write the missing words.

1 What ___**are you**___ doing?

  I ___**'m looking**___ for my jacket.

2 What _____ Lucy doing?

  She _____ sailing a boat.

3 What _____ you _____?

  I _____ for a bus.

4 What's Ben doing?

  He _____ with his cars.

5 _____ Marie doing?

  _____ her bike.

6 _____ Dad doing?

  _____ the guitar.

Reading: a postcard

1 Read the postcards. Tick ☑ the activities that Ryan and Dan do. Write *R* (Ryan), *D* (Dan) or *B* (both).

☑ **B** swim   ☐ ride a bike   ☐ sail a boat

☐ look for shells   ☐ skateboard   ☐ play football

☐ visit the beach   ☐ climb trees   ☐ take photos

Hi Ryan

I'm visiting my grandma in Italy. We visit her every year and we come by plane. Grandma lives by the sea and she's even got a swimming pool too, so I'm swimming every day! When I'm here I like riding my bike and looking for shells on the beach. I've got a friend called Mario and his dad has got a boat. I'd like to sail the boat but I can't – the boat is big!

What are you doing this holiday?

Write to me!

Dan

Hi Dan

I'm at home for the holiday but I'm doing lots of fun things. I'm playing football with my friends, skateboarding in the park and visiting the beach with my mum and my sister (we're swimming and looking for shells). I'd like to go to Italy and eat pizza and ice cream! Are you eating pizza? When we visit my grandma we go by train – she lives in the city. She hasn't got a swimming pool but she's got a big garden. I like climbing trees and taking photos.

See you soon!

Ryan

1 What do you like doing on holiday? What would you like to do? Make notes.

I like _____
_____
_____
_____

I'd like to _____
_____
_____
_____

2 Write a postcard to Dan. Write about what you are doing on holiday.

Listening: transport

1 🎧 **15** Listen and tick ☑ the correct picture.

1
a ✓
b

2
a
b

3
a
b

4
a
b

5
a
b

6
a
b

2 🎧 **16** Listen and circle the correct answers.

1 How does Amelia want to go to China?
 a By boat. **b** By plane.

2 Who wants to walk to the sports centre?
 a Emma's dad. **b** Emma.

3 What is Ronnie doing?
 a He's playing a computer game.
 b He's playing football.

4 What is Ruby doing?
 a She's reading a book. **b** She's watching TV.

5 How does Oscar get to school?
 a By car. **b** By bus.

6 Which bus stops next to Laura's house?
 a Number twenty. **b** Number twelve.

1 Look at the photos and mime the actions.
Play the guessing game.

> Number 2! You're driving a car.

> Yes, I am!

canoe

car

hot air balloon

train

rocket

motorbike

2 Think of an amazing place to visit. Complete the sentences.

MY AMAZING PLACE

I'd like to go to _____.
I'd like to travel with _____.
I'd like to travel by _____.

3 Talk about your amazing place.

> I'd like to go to London. I'd like to travel with my mum, my dad and my brother. I'd like to travel by hot air balloon!

8 ing forms

Dancing is great.

Playing volleyball is difficult.

Swimming is fun.

Watching TV is boring.

Language focus

Use **verb** + **ing** to make sentences describing activities.

Riding is great.

Flying a kite is difficult.

1 Circle the correct words to complete the sentences.

1 (*Flying*) / *Fly* a kite is difficult.

2 *Play* / *Playing* computer games is boring.

3 *Making* / *Makes* cakes is fun.

4 *Riding* / *Ride* a horse is easy.

5 *Reads* / *Reading* a book is great.

6 *Painting* / *Paint* pictures is fun.

2 **Write the words to complete the sentences.**

①

Playing baseball
is boring.

②

_____
is great.

③

_____
is fun.

④

_____
is difficult.

⑤

_____
is fun.

⑥

_____
is difficult.

3 **Complete the dialogue with the words from the box.**

club   Playing   ~~join~~   Dancing   swimming   boring

Sally Let's **(1)** _____**join**_____ a club.

Bob That's a great idea. What do you think about dancing?

Sally **(2)** _____ is difficult. I'd like to join the **(3)** _____ club.
What about you?

Bob No. Swimming is **(4)** _____.

Sally I think I'll join the football **(5)** _____. You can have fun with
your friends.

Bob OK. **(6)** _____ football is great.

Like + ing

Language focus

Use **What ... like doing?** to ask about what activities other people like. Use **I like** + **verb** + **ing** to answer. Use **So do I**, **Me too** and **I don't** to give positive and negative short answers.

What sport do you *like doing?*

I like swimming.   *So do I. / Me too.*

I like playing football.   *I don't.*

1 **Match the sentences with the pictures.**

1 I like swimming.

  So do I.   [c]

2 I like playing football.

  I don't.   [   ]

3 I like running.

  So do I.   [   ]

4 I like playing table tennis.

  I don't.   [   ]

8

2 **Circle the correct words to complete the dialogue.**

Matt What sport do you like **(1)** do / (doing)?

Jane I like playing hockey.

Matt I **(2)** *don't like* / *don't.* I like dancing – I think dancing is great. Do you like any other sports?

Jane Yes, I like **(3)** *rides* / *riding* my bike on a sunny day.

Matt So **(4)** *do I* / *I do.* I **(5)** *am like* / *like* going to the lake on my bike and swimming.

Jane Me **(6)** *to* / *too*!

3 **Look and complete the sentences.**

1

✓ I **like playing tennis**____.

✓ So **do I**_____.

2

✓ I _____.

✗ I _____.

3

✓ I _____.

✓ Me _____.

4

What sport _____?

_____

Reading: a text message

1 Read the messages. Circle the correct words to complete the sentences.

CHATS School friends	*Matt, Sally, Ben, You*

Saturday 25 June

I'm at the park at a football club. Playing football in the park is fun! 11:32 ✓✓

Sally Jones
Hi! Football is my favourite sport. Is it for boys and girls? Can I come too? **11:35**

Matt Brown
Me too! Where are you? **11:40**

Ben Hardy
I don't like football. Football is boring. I'm playing tennis. See you later. **11:42**

I'm at the town park near the cinema. There are twenty boys and girls here. It's on Saturday mornings at eleven o'clock. Come and join us. We are playing in between the ice cream shop and the little playground. We're wearing blue T-shirts and yellow shorts. 11:45 ✓✓

Sally Jones
I love that ice cream shop! I can't come today. I'm swimming with my sister. Bye! **11:48**

1 You are at the *swimming pool* / (*park*).

2 Sally *doesn't like* / *likes* football.

3 Matt *doesn't like* / *likes* football.

4 Ben is playing *football* / *tennis*.

5 There are *twenty* / *eleven* children playing football at the park.

6 Sally is *at the swimming pool* / *eating an ice cream*.

1 Plan a conversation.

Who are you chatting with? _____

Where are you? _____

Where are your friends? _____

What are you doing? _____

2 Write your conversation.

CHATS School friends

Listening: let's play!

1 🎧 17 **Listen and match the children with the sports they like playing.**

1 Chloe

2 Noah

3 Jess

4 Lucas

5 Esme

6 Ethan

2 🎧 18 **Listen and circle *yes* or *no*.**

1 Tom plays football on Fridays.	(yes)/ no
2 Tom plays football at a football club.	yes / no
3 On Saturdays, Tom goes swimming with his friends.	yes / no
4 For Tom, swimming is boring.	yes / no
5 Tom plays table tennis on Sundays.	yes / no
6 Tom has got a new tennis racket.	yes / no

1 **Work with a friend. What is the equipment? Look, choose and say.**

> Number 5.

> They're goggles.

| goal | board | racket | helmet | pitch | goggles | bat | net |

①

②

③

④

⑤

⑥

⑦

⑧

2 **With your friend, think of sports that need the equipment in Activity 1. Play the guessing game.**

> Do you need a racket?

> Yes, you do.

> Is it tennis?

> No, it isn't.

> Is it badminton?

> Yes, it is!

3 **Create a sport and draw it. Complete and practise.**

The name of my sport is _____.

You play my sport in / on _____.

For my sport, you need _____.

4 **Talk about your sport.**

> The name of my sport is hotball. You play hotball on a court. For my sport, you need two balls and a net.

9 Can for requests

Can we go hiking this weekend?

Can I go to Lucy's house to listen to music this afternoon?

Can we eat pizza for dinner tomorrow evening?

Language focus

Use **Can I / we** + **verb** to make requests.

Can I go horse riding tomorrow morning?

Can we visit Grandpa and Grandma in the afternoon?

---

1 **Match to complete the sentences.**

1 Can I

2 Can I visit

3 Can we

4 Can I go

5 Can we have

6 Can we take

a my cousin at the weekend?

b horse riding tomorrow afternoon?

c pizza for dinner?

d go camping in the summer?

e my football to the park?

f help you in the garden?

2 Complete the dialogues with the words from the box.

| help | visit | ~~what~~ | have | Can | We |

Dad Tom, **(1)** _____**what**_____ would you like to do on Saturday?

Tom **(2)** _____ we go to the park in the afternoon?

Dad Fine. What about you, Lucy? What would you like to do?

Lucy Can I **(3)** _____ Grandma in the afternoon? I want to **(4)** _____ her in the garden.

Dad OK. **(5)** _____ can go to the park in the morning and to Grandma's in the afternoon. What do you want to eat for dinner?

Tom and Lucy Can we **(6)** _____ pizza?

Dad Yes!

3 Write questions using *Can I* or *Can we* and the words from the box.

| build a tree house | have pizza | ~~have a party~~ |
| go horse riding | visit Grandpa | go swimming |

1 **Can we have a party** this weekend?

4 _____ for dinner tomorrow afternoon?

2 _____ tomorrow morning?

5 _____ tomorrow morning?

3 _____ tomorrow afternoon?

6 _____ tomorrow afternoon?

Revision

Language focus

Use **Do** or **Have** to ask Yes/No questions. Use **Can ... ?** to ask about ability. Use question words (**Where** / **Whose**) to ask questions.

Does *your sister eat tomatoes?*   *Yes, she does.*

Have *spiders got eight legs?*   *Yes, they have.*

Can *you swim?*   *No, I can't.*

Where *are my pencils?*   *On the desk.*

Whose *jumper is pink?*   *Emily's.*

① **Read and write the question words.**

1 ___Does___ your brother like apples? Yes, he does.

2 _____ you sing? Yes, I can.

3 _____ you got a go-kart? No, I haven't.

4 _____ your mum get up at six o'clock? No, she doesn't.

5 _____ bag is this? It's Dan's.

2 Write questions.

1 hiking / Mark / Does / like / ? **Does Mark like hiking?**

2 socks / these / Whose / are / ? _____

3 horse riding / Can / go / tomorrow / we / ? _____

4 your / a lot / Does / sleep / cat / ? _____

5 toy shop / the / Where / is / ? _____

6 your / a cinema / town / Has / got / ? _____

3 Complete the questions.

1 ___**Can you play**___ volleyball? No, I can't.

2 _____ a train station?
Yes, it has.

3 _____ dancing? Yes, I do.

4 _____ my pens and pencils?
They're in your pencil case.

5 _____ book
_____ ? It's not mine. It's May's.

6 _____ any cheese? No, we haven't.

Reading: a story

1   **Read the story. Answer the questions.**

1 How old is Cinderella? **She is young.**

2 Who does she live with? _____

3 What time is the party? _____

4 Whose party is it? _____

5 Can the prince find Cinderella? _____

6 Whose feet are the right size for the shoe? _____

Cinderella is a fairy tale about a young girl. She's got blue eyes and blonde hair. She lives with her two ugly sisters and her wicked stepmother. She gets up early and cleans the house every day. One day she gets a party invitation. It says:

> Come to a party at the palace on Saturday. It starts at seven o'clock.
>
> Prince Harry

Cinderella asks her wicked stepmother, 'Can I go to the party?' but her stepmother says, 'No, you can't.'

But Cinderella has got a fairy godmother. She helps Cinderella get a dress and she helps her get to the party.

Cinderella is wearing a beautiful dress and shoes. She meets Prince Harry at the party. At twelve o'clock Cinderella goes home. She runs and she has only one shoe. The prince says, 'Where is Cinderella?'

The next day the prince looks for Cinderella but he can't find her. He looks all around town. He has got Cinderella's shoe and he asks the girls in town to try on the shoe.

He goes to Cinderella's house and her sisters try on the shoe. Their feet aren't small, but the shoe is. Cinderella tries on the shoe and it fits! Hooray!

Cinderella and the prince live happily ever after.

1 **Put the sentences in order to make the story of Sleeping Beauty, a princess who lives in a palace.**

a The wicked witch isn't invited. She is angry. ☐

b When Sleeping Beauty is 16, she pricks her finger on a spinning wheel. ☐

c A prince finds her. The people in the palace wake up. ☐

d She and everyone in the palace sleep for 100 years. ☐

e The wicked witch says, 'She will prick her finger and die.' ☐

f A forest grows around the palace. ☐

g Sleeping Beauty is a baby. Her parents have a birthday party for her. 1

2 **Use the sentences from Activity 1 to write the story of Sleeping Beauty.**

When Sleeping Beauty is a baby _____

_____

_____

_____

_____

_____

_____

_____

_____

_____

_____

They all live happily ever after.

Listening: fun on holidays

1 🎧 19 **What can Edward do at summer camp?**
Listen and tick ☑ or cross ☒.

This week at summer camp!

Take riding lessons.	☑
Build a tree house.	☐
Swim in the river.	☐
Watch TV.	☐
Go fishing.	☐
Go hiking.	☐
Play volleyball and tennis.	☐
Help in the garden.	☐

2 🎧 20 **Listen and circle the correct answers.**

1 What does Mila want to do now?

ⓐ Go to the beach.

b Have lunch.

2 Whose house is it?

a It's Mila's house.

b It's Grandpa's house.

3 How many bedrooms are there?

a Five.

b Four.

4 Has the house got a garden?

a Yes, it has.

b No, it hasn't.

5 Can Mila go hiking tomorrow?

a Yes, she can.

b No, she can't.

6 Who wants to help in the kitchen?

a Mila's cousins.

b Mila.

1 Imagine you are at a summer camp. Tick ☑ five things you can do. Then ask a friend and tick ☑ what you can do at their camp.

> Can you take riding lessons at your summer camp?

> Yes, you can.

● SUMMER CAMP

You can ...	My camp	My friend's camp
take riding lessons		
build a tree house		
swim		
watch TV		
bake cakes		
do sports		
ride a bike		
read books		
go hiking		
visit new places		

2 Choose one thing from Activity 1 that you and your friend can do at your camps. Draw a picture of you and your friend.

3 Talk about your picture.

> Look, this is me and Liam. We're at summer camp. We're building a tree house!

Audioscripts

Welcome Unit page 10

1 **Boy** Hello! This is my new classroom. Come and look. This is the board! We've got a big board!

2 **Boy** There's a nice clock on the wall. It's red. Can you see it?

3 **Boy** This is the teacher's desk. Look, there are some rulers on the desk.

4 **Boy** Can you see the bookcase? There are some books in it. I want to read them!

5 **Boy** This is my desk. I sit here with my friend, Ben. There are two chairs: one chair for me and one chair for Ben.

6 **Boy** Look! This is my new pencil case. There are some crayons in my pencil case. My crayons are new, too!

Miss White Good morning, everyone!

Children Good morning, Miss White.

Miss White It's nice to see you all again! Do you like the new classroom?

Children Yes, we do!

Miss White Me too! OK! Oh no, don't sit down. Don't sit down, please. Stand up. Stand up, please. Can you get your books? Get your books, please. That's great. Now, open your books at page one. Oh no, don't get your crayons. Don't get your crayons. Get a pencil and write your name. Write your name, please. That's very good. Well done, class!

Unit 1 page 18

Hello! I'm Lucy and I've got a big sister, Eva. I love my big sister. Do you want to know about her day? OK. Eva gets up at six o'clock. Six o'clock is early! Then she gets dressed and helps Mum to make breakfast. Eva has breakfast at seven o'clock. After breakfast, she brushes her teeth and puts her books in her bag. At eight o'clock, Eva goes to school. Then she has lunch at one o'clock. Chicken and carrots are her favourite! After school, Eva plays with me. Then we have dinner together at seven o'clock, and we go to bed at nine o'clock. In bed, Eva and I talk about our day. That's one of my favourite things!

Teacher OK, it's your turn, Dan. When do you get home from school?

Dan I get home at four o'clock. I walk home with my mum and my brother. My dad's at work.

Teacher That sounds nice. And what do you do at home?

Dan I play with my brother. Then, at five o'clock we go to the park. I play in the park with friends.

Teacher That's good! And when do you have dinner?

Dan Hmm … Well, I get home from the park at seven o'clock, and I have dinner at eight o'clock. After dinner, my brother and I read a story with my dad. We like stories!

Teacher A story after dinner is great! And then do you go to bed?

Dan No, I don't! I brush my teeth, and then I go to bed.

Teacher Oh, of course, Dan! Well done!

Unit 2 page 26

Hello! Today, I'm at the zoo with my friends! There's Alex. He's with the tigers. Alex loves tigers. Oh, look. That's Grace. Grace likes tigers too, but her favourite animal is the hippo. For Grace, hippos are fantastic! Now, can you see the crocodiles? My friend Tom is next to them. Tom likes crocodiles a lot. And that's my friend Kim. Kim likes crocodiles too, but snakes are her favourite animal. Kim likes all snakes, long or short, big or small! And my friend Jill is there, with the zebras. Zebras are Jill's favourite animal. OK, what about me? I'm Nick and I love polar bears! Polar bears are amazing!

Tony Hello, Holly!

Holly Oh! Hi, Tony!

Tony Are you here with your family?

Holly Yes, I am. We really like the zoo.

Tony I like it, too. The crocodiles are amazing!

Holly Yes! My mum really likes crocodiles. They're her favourite. My dad doesn't like crocodiles. He loves zebras. Zebras are my dad's favourite animals.

Tony Zebras are nice! What about your brother? What's his favourite animal?

Holly Well, my brother likes snakes! Arghh!

Tony Haha! I love snakes, too. They're cool!

Holly No, they're not! I don't like snakes, and my sister doesn't like snakes. They're ugly!

Tony OK, OK. Hey, do you like parrots, Holly? They're my favourite.

Holly Hmm … not really. I don't like parrots, Tony. I like monkeys! Monkeys are funny!

Unit 3 page 34

Sam Do you like your town, Hugo?

Hugo Yes, I do! It's great. Do you like your town, Sam?

Sam Yes. My town is very nice. It's got a new café! Has your town got a café, Hugo?

Hugo Yes, it has. It's called the Blue Café. We go there for breakfast at the weekend.

Sam   Cool! My town has got a big cinema. Has your town got a cinema?

Hugo   No, it hasn't. There isn't a cinema in my town.

Sam   Then come to my town! And I can go to the swimming pool in your town, Hugo.

Hugo   That's right, Sam. My town's got a great swimming pool!

Sam   Yes, it's fun! My town hasn't got a swimming pool. But it's got a big playground.

Hugo   My town has got a big playground, too. It's next to the train station. Has your town got a train station, Sam?

Sam   No, it hasn't. There isn't a train station in my town. I can go to your town by car!

Hugo   Good idea!

1 Boy   Hello. Can you help me, please?

   Girl   Yes, of course.

   Boy   Where's the bookshop?

   Girl   It's next to the clothes shop.

   Boy   OK, next to the clothes shop. Thanks!

2 Girl   Hi, Eric. We're at the bus station.

   Eric   Where's the bus station?

   Girl   It's behind the museum.

   Eric   Behind the museum. OK. See you soon!

3 Boy   Where's the zoo, May?

   May   Hmm … let's look at the map. The zoo is in front of the school.

   Boy   Great! Let's go!

4 Girl   Hello. Do you know the monument?

   Boy   Yes, I do.

   Girl   Where is it?

   Boy   It's on the hill. Look!

   Girl   Yes! I can see it on the hill!

5 Boy   Are you at the sports centre, Sophie?

   Sophie   Yes, I am.

   Boy   Is it behind the car park?

   Sophie   No, it's next to the car park.

   Boy   Next to the car park? OK, see you there!

Unit 4 page 42

1 Polly   What is there in the cupboard, Tim?

   Tim   There are some potatoes.

   Polly   Some potatoes? Is that all? Let's go to the market!

2 Tim   Would you like an egg sandwich, Polly?

   Polly   Yes, please! Are there any eggs?

   Tim   Yes, there are some eggs in the fridge.

3 Polly   Are there any lemons, Tim?

   Tim   Yes, there are. How many lemons would you like?

   Polly   Hmm … I'd like three lemons, please.

4 Polly   OK. We need some vegetables for the salad.

   Tim   Look! There are some beans in the fridge.

   Polly   That's right! We've got lots of beans!

5 Tim   What's your favourite fruit, Polly?

   Polly   Hmm … I love watermelon.

   Tim   Great. Would you like some watermelon after lunch?

   Polly   Yes, please!

6 Polly   Tim, would you like some pizza?

   Tim   Yes, good idea!

   Polly   OK. We've got some cheese. Are there any tomatoes?

   Tim   Yes, there are. The tomatoes are on the table – look.

   Polly   OK, great!

1 Dad   Would you like a kiwi, Lucy?

   Lucy   Hmm. No thanks, Dad. Are there any grapes?

   Dad   Yes, there are.

   Lucy   I'd like some grapes, please.

2 Mum   Would you like an apple, Connor?

   Connor   No, thank you, Mum. Can I have a kiwi?

   Mum   Let's see … Oh, yes, there's a kiwi here. Here you are.

   Connor   Thanks, Mum.

3 Anna   Where's my lunchbox, Dad?

   Dad   I don't know, Anna. What would you like?

   Anna   My apple. Oh, my lunchbox is here. And here's my apple!

   Dad   Good!

4 Mum   Jack?

   Jack   Yes, Mum.

   Mum   Can you help me, please? I can't find the mangoes.

   Jack   Look, Mum. The mangoes are in the fridge. Would you like one?

   Mum   Yes, please!

5 Dad   Are you sure, May?

   May   Yes, Dad. I'd like some for breakfast. Please!

   Dad   OK. Let's take it. It's a big watermelon!

   May   Thanks, Dad. I like watermelon!

Unit 5 page 50

1 Milly   Wow! These mirrors are lovely!

   Mum   Yes! Would you like this blue mirror or that orange mirror?

   Milly   I'd like this blue mirror. Thanks, Mum.

2 Milly   There are lots of wardrobes, Mum!

   Mum   Yes, there are. What about this one, Milly?

   Milly   Hmm … It's nice, but it's very small.

   Mum   OK. Let's get that wardrobe. It's big!

   Milly   Good idea!

3 Milly   I like those rugs, Mum!

   Mum   Me too. Do you want the red one or the green one?

   Milly   Can we get the red rug, please?

   Mum   Of course! Red is your favourite colour!

4 Milly   Look at these lamps! The yellow lamp is ugly.

   Mum   Yes, it is. What about this white lamp?

   Milly   I like this white lamp! It's nice for my new bedroom!

5	Mum	Look at these sofas, Milly. I like this purple sofa.
	Milly	I like the purple sofa too, Mum. The brown sofa isn't very nice.
6	Milly	Mum, can we get a poster of an animal for my bedroom?
	Mum	Good idea. Look at the crocodile!
	Milly	It's cool, but I love the tiger.
	Mum	OK, let's get the poster of the tiger!

 12

Dad	Look at this bedroom! You two need to tidy up.
Children	Sorry, Dad.
Dad	Whose ball is this?
Adam	That's Lucy's ball.
Dad	Can you put your ball in the box, please, Lucy?
Lucy	OK, Dad.
Dad	Whose crayons are these?
Adam	They're Lucy's crayons too, Dad.
Dad	OK. Lucy, put your crayons in the pencil case, please. Now, jeans! Are these your jeans too, Lucy?
Lucy	No, they're Adam's jeans.
Dad	Put your jeans in the wardrobe, please, Adam.
Adam	OK.
Dad	And Adam … your jacket's on the chair again!
Adam	That's Lucy's jacket, Dad.
Lucy	Oh! Sorry! Yes, it's my jacket. I can put it in the wardrobe.
Dad	Well done. Now, whose books are these, Lucy?
Lucy	They're Adam's books, Dad.
Dad	Adam, put these books on your desk, please.
Adam	OK. But Lucy's kite is on my desk, Dad. Look.
Dad	Lucy's kite? Lucy, your kite goes in the box!
Lucy	OK, Dad.
Dad	Well done, children! Now you've got a tidy bedroom again!

Unit 6 page 58

 13

1	Grace	Happy birthday, Jill! What time is your party?
	Jill	Thanks, Grace! It's at five o'clock. I'm very excited!
2	Dad	Are you OK, Jenny?
	Jenny	Dad, the party's great. But I'm very tired now.
	Dad	You're tired and it's late. Let's go home.
3	Max	I'm very happy, Leah!
	Leah	Why?
	Max	Look. I've got new glasses for my birthday.
	Leah	Oh, yes! Your new glasses are cool, Max!
4	Kate	Henry, are you OK?
	Henry	No, I'm not. I'm very angry. Look. Carmen's party is on Friday and my party is on Friday, too!
	Kate	Oh dear!
5	Mum	Oliver, are you scared?
	Oliver	Yes, Mum. I'm scared. I don't like that big spider …
	Mum	Oh, don't worry, Oliver. The spider is Dad!
6	Beth	Dad, it's Jamie's party today …

Dad	That's great, Beth. But you look sad.
Beth	I am sad. Jamie's party is in the park, and it's raining!
Dad	Oh, I see!

 14

Hello, my name's Alice. I love birthday parties. They're fun! We can play with our friends and eat cake. This year, there are lots of parties in my class, and they are all different. Alex and Dan's party is in January. Their party is at our town's new cinema. They're very excited! Then we've got Kim's party in March. She's very happy, too. Kim's party is at her family's farm! I love animals! Now, Pat and Mark's birthdays are in April, and their party is at the sports centre! They like playing sports. Then Bobby's party is in May. It's at the Sunshine Café. We love the cake there! And lastly, my party is with my friend Olivia. Our birthdays are in June, and our party is in the park!

Unit 7 page 66

 15

1	Girl	Look, Michael – I'm flying my plane. What are you doing? Are you flying your helicopter?
	Michael	No, I'm not. Look – I'm flying my plane, too!
2	Boy	Come on, Kelly. Let's go! We can take our skateboards.
	Kelly	I don't want to go by skateboard. I'd like to go by bike.
	Boy	OK! Let's take our bikes!
3	Boy	Mum, I'd like to take the train to the cinema.
	Mum	Me too. But the train doesn't stop at the cinema. Let's take the bus.
	Boy	OK. Let's go by bus.
4	Girl	Would you like to ride a motorbike, Nick?
	Nick	Hmm … I'm not sure. Motorbikes are very big. I'd like to ride a scooter.
	Girl	Really?
	Nick	Yes. My scooter is great!
5	Boy	Does your dad drive a lorry, Ava?
	Ava	No, he doesn't.
	Boy	What does he drive?
	Ava	My dad drives a taxi.
6	Girl	Look, Tom! Would you like to get on that big ship or on that little boat?
	Tom	I'd like to get on that little boat.
	Girl	Why?
	Tom	Little boats are fun!

 16

1	Boy	Look at all these countries, Amelia. Where would you like to go?
	Amelia	I'd like to go to China.
	Boy	Well, you'd need to take a plane.
	Amelia	Not a plane – I'd like to go to China by boat!
	Boy	By boat? Wow! But China is far!
2	Emma	Dad, can we ride our bikes to the sports centre?
	Dad	That's a nice idea, but there are lots of cars on the road, Emma. Let's walk.
	Emma	Oh, Dad. I don't want to walk …
	Dad	Come on, Emma. We can walk fast! The sports centre isn't far.

3	**Lola**	Hi, Ronnie.
	Ronnie	Oh, hi, Lola.
	Lola	What are you doing?
	Ronnie	I'm playing a computer game. It's about cars!
	Lola	Would you like to play football with me?
	Ronnie	OK. When I finish my game.
4	**Ruby**	Hello, Ted.
	Ted	Hi, Ruby. What are you doing?
	Ruby	I'm watching TV. What about you?
	Ted	I'm reading a book about planes. It's amazing!
5	**Girl**	Do you go to school by car, Oscar?
	Oscar	No, I don't.
	Girl	Do you walk?
	Oscar	No, I don't. I go to school by bus.
6	**Ben**	How do I get to your house, Laura?
	Laura	Take the bus, Ben.
	Ben	The number twelve bus?
	Laura	No, take the number twenty. The twenty stops next to my house.
	Ben	OK!

Unit 8 page 74

1	**Boy**	Do you like playing baseball, Chloe?
	Chloe	Yes, I love baseball! It's fun!
2	**Girl**	Noah, would you like to play table tennis with me?
	Noah	Yes, of course! Playing table tennis is great!
3	**Boy**	What sports do you like, Jess?
	Jess	Well, I like playing one sport. You play it with a racket – guess.
	Boy	That's easy! Tennis.
	Jess	No, I like playing badminton!
4	**Girl**	What do you think about football, Lucas?
	Lucas	Playing football is boring! I like playing volleyball.
	Girl	Me too. Playing volleyball is fun.
5	**Boy**	OK. We can play hockey or football, Esme.
	Esme	Playing hockey is difficult. I like football.
	Boy	OK! Let's play football!
6	**Girl**	Are you ready for the game, Ethan?
	Ethan	Yes, I am! I love playing hockey! Hockey's my favourite sport!

Hello! I'm Tom and I love doing sport. It's great! On Fridays, I play football with my friends. We go to a football club. We wear red T-shirts at our football club. On Saturdays, I go swimming with my family. Swimming is fun! There's a new swimming pool next to my house and I love it. On Sundays, I play table tennis with my brother. Playing table tennis is easy! Oh, and I play tennis, too! There's a nice tennis court in the park in our town. I like playing on it. Oh, I can show you my new tennis racket. It's purple and blue! Look!

Unit 9 page 82

Edward	Mr Thompson, can I ask you some questions about summer camp?
Mr Thompson	Yes, of course you can, Edward.
Edward	OK. Can I take riding lessons this week?
Mr Thompson	Yes, you can. You can take riding lessons every morning with Ellie. She's very friendly.
Edward	Great! And can I build a tree house?
Mr Thompson	Good news, Edward. You can build a tree house tomorrow morning!
Edward	That's fun! You know, I really like swimming. Can I go swimming in the river?
Mr Thompson	Sorry, you can't swim in the river, Edward. But you can swim in our swimming pool.
Edward	OK. And can I watch TV this week?
Mr Thompson	Oh, no, you can't. We haven't got TVs at the camp! There are lots of things to do outside – you can go fishing and hiking this week.
Edward	Well, fishing and hiking are OK … Hmm … Can I play volleyball and tennis, too?
Mr Thompson	No, you can't. Not this week. But you can help in the garden.
Edward	OK. I like helping!

Mila	I love this house, Mum. Look out of the window – there's the sea. It's big. It's amazing!
Mum	Yes, it is, Mila!
Mila	Can we go to the beach now?
Mum	Hmm … Not now. Let's have lunch. We can go to the beach after that. OK?
Mila	OK!
Mum	You know, Grandpa's very happy – you, me and your cousins are staying in his house.
Mila	Yes, I like being in Grandpa's beach house. And I like playing with my cousins!
Mum	I can see that!
Mila	Grandpa's house is big, Mum. How many bedrooms are there? Four or five?
Mum	Four. There are four bedrooms.
Mila	My favourite place in the house is the garden.
Mum	Yes, the garden is lovely. Would you like to help Grandpa in the garden this week?
Mila	Yes, of course! I'd like that. And Mum, can we go hiking tomorrow?
Mum	Yes, of course we can. We can go with your cousins. Now, what about lunch? Can you help me make it?
Mila	Yes! I love helping in the garden and I love helping in the kitchen!

Acknowledgements

The authors and publishers acknowledge the following sources of copyright material and are grateful for the permissions granted. While every effort has been made, it has not always been possible to identify the sources of all the material used, or to trace all copyright holders. If any omissions are brought to our notice, we will be happy to include the appropriate acknowledgements on reprinting and in the next update to the digital edition, as applicable.

Key: ST = Starter, U = Unit

Photography

The following images are sourced from Getty Images.

ST: recep-bg/E+; goldenKB/iStock/Getty Images Plus; **U1:** Comstock Images/Stockbyte; Studiocartoon/iStock/ GettyImages Plus; Wavebreakmedia Ltd/Getty Images Plus; **U2:** Dinodia Photo/The Image Bank Unreleased; Marka/Universal Images Group; wilpunt/iStock/Getty Images Plus; Skyler Ewing/EyeEm; real444/iStock/Getty Images Plus; Juanmonino/iStock/Getty Images Plus; Nophamon Yanyapong/EyeEm; ValuaVitaly/iStock/Getty Images Plus; nattanan726/iStock/Getty Images Plus; DrPAS/iStock/Getty Images Plus; anankkml/iStock/ Getty Images Plus; zokru/iStock/Getty Images Plus; VitalisG/iStock/Getty Images Plus; AaronAmat/iStock/ Getty Images Plus; Image Source/Vetta; Kuntalee Rangnoi/iStock/Getty Images Plus; Andreas Speich/EyeEm; Js Photography/Moment; Piotr Pestka/500px; WLDavies/iStock/Getty Images Plus; Razvan Ciuca/Moment; FatCamera/E+; **U3:** selimaksan/E+; Jose Luis Pelaez Inc/DigitalVision; Lena Granefelt; **U4:** alex5248/iStock/ Getty Images Plus; Devonyu/iStock/Getty Images Plus; kbwills/iStock/Getty Images Plus; Kangah/iStock/Getty Images Plus; Scrambled/iStock/Getty Images Plus; Paola Zucchi/Photolibrary/Getty Images Plus; Moncherie/ E+; Jose Luis Pelaez Inc/DigitalVision; Soldt/iStock/Getty Images Plus; Juanmonino/E+; ozgurdonmaz/iStock/ Getty Images Plus; Jodie Griggs/Moment; SvetlanaK/iStock/Getty Images Plus; subjug/iStock/Getty Images Plus; Natthakan Jommanee/EyeEm; Jamakosy/iStock/Getty Images Plus; pjohnson1/E+; Imgorthand/E+; **U5:** Stephanie Hager - HagerPhoto/Stockbyte; irina88w/iStock/Getty Images Plus; Maskot; Iwan Chorniy/ iStock/Getty Images Plus; cyfrogclone/DigitalVision Vectors; **U6:** David Marsden/Photolibrary/Getty Images Plus; Creativ Studio Heinemann; 130920/Moment; Tolimir/E+; Craig Tuttle/Corbis Historical; View Pictures/Universal Images Group; Alain BENAINOUS/Gamma-Rapho; kali9/E+; **U7:** pikenpri foto/Moment; MHJ/DigitalVision Vectors; Oscar Porras González/500px/500Px Plus; Cassandra Kosmayer/EyeEm; James Hipps/EyeEm; New SIGHT Photography/iStock/Getty Images Plus; Stocktrek Images; Henn Photography/ Cultura; Rakdee/DigitalVision Vectors; Matriyoshka/iStock/Getty Images Plus; **U8:** Cybernesco/iStock/Getty Images Plus; carlosalvarez/E+; Goodboy Picture Company/E+; Layland Masuda/Moment Open; Elena Riim/ EyeEm; Daniel MacDonald/www.dmacphoto.com/Moment; fstop123/iStock/Getty Images Plus; Stockbyte; Andersen Ross Photography Inc/DigitalVision; Tim Macpherson/Cultura; ddukang/iStock/Getty Images Plus; freestylephoto/iStock/Getty Images Plus; artisteer/iStock/Getty Images Plus; Thomas Northcut/Photodisc; Viruj/iStock/Getty Images Plus; Nerthuz/iStock/Getty Images Plus; ZargonDesign/E+; Bim/E+; **U9:** Imgorthand/ E+; Jupiterimages/Creatas; wundervisuals/E+.

The following images are sourced from another library.

U4: Andy Tu/Shutterstock; U8: Mike Flippo/Shutterstock; tkemot/Shutterstock.

Commissioned photography by Stephen Bond.

Illustrations

Clive Goodyer (Beehive Illustration); Anna Hancock (Beehive Illustration); Andrew Hennessy; Marek Jagucki; Chris Lensch; Daniel Limon (Beehive Illustration); Bernice Lum; Andy Parker; Alan Rowe (Beehive Illustration); David Russell; David Semple.

Audio

Audio production by Hart McLeod.

Typeset

EMC Design limited.

Cover design by We Are Bold.